"String Along with Me"

A Collector's Guide To

Stringholders

by
Sharon Ray Jacobs

photographs by
Sharon Ray Jacobs

Copyright 1996
Sharon Ray Jacobs

ISBN#: 0-89538-042-0

Printed by IMAGE GRAPHICS, INC., Paducah, Kentucky

Published by
L-W Book Sales
P.O. Box 69
Gas City, IN 46933

CONTENTS

DEDICATION

This book is dedicated to stringholder collectors everywhere.

ACKNOWLEDGMENTS

I would like to thank Marc and Sherri Solochek, Bruce Shrinsky, Emma and Louis Kretchek, Ron at Webb's Antique Mall, Lois and Ralph Behm, Fran and Robin Hoffer, Margie and Dan Kaplan, Paul Shaw, Suzan Dentry, Al Little, and Linda Laughlin for allowing me to photograph their stringholders for this book.

I also wish to thank Helen Yeutter and Ed Lehew, for submitting photos for this book. John Reece, Susan Chapin, and Michael Jacobs provided valuable leads for which I am very grateful. And to all the stringholder collectors who have ever given me information concerning the history and pricing of stringholders, thank you.

A special thanks to Mike's Camera in Boulder, Colorado for all their advice and custom film development.

Without these contributors this book would have been impossible to complete.

HISTORY

Stringholders were developed to assist merchants and manufacturers in dispensing untangled string to tie packages in the days before paper bags and scotch tape. The earliest stringholders were made of cast iron, with patents dating back to the 1860's.

By the late 1800's , stringholders were also seen in homes, still made of cast iron, but also in wood and glass in more decorative designs. String was used in the home for packaging as well as in food preparation. Cooks today still use string to truss their chickens and turkeys.

Advertising stringholders were seen in general stores, advertising such products as shoes, soap, and pickles. They were generally made of cast iron or tin. Currently, advertising stringholders command high prices. A tin Heinz 57 pickle is valued at $8,250 in today's market, while a painted cast iron stringholder advertising Red Goose Shoes is valued at $9,350.

Gorham Silver Company made stringholders in sterling silver while some depression glass companies also made them to go with their lines of glassware. Hull Pottery made a Little Red Riding Hood stringholder now valued between $2,800 and $3,200. A rare and expensive find!

Stringholders of human faces, animals and fruits were introduced in the late 1920's and the 1930's to add a more decorative touch to the kitchen. They were produced in ceramic and chalkware. Chalkware is plaster of paris, usually painted with watercolors. These decorative stringholders were sold in dime stores for between 19 and 69 cents and common in kitchens until the early 1950's.

This book deals primarily with the stringholders most popular with collectors, the figural stringholders made between the 1920's and the 1950's.

Advertising Pickle Stringholder,
tin, (Pure Foods, Heinz).
$8,250

MANUFACTURERS

Most stringholders have no manufacturer's marks on them, and the ones that do, little or nothing is known about the company.

Stringholders were made primarily in the United States and Japan. Universal Statuary Company is a mark found on some chalkware stringholders. Universal Statuary is still in business in Chicago, although they have not produced statuary in chalkware for decades. (They now use resins.) Universal was sold several times since the 1940's and all stringholder molds and records have been discarded. The marking, H. Bello, also seen on chalk stringholders, was an artist for Universal Statuary. Universal Statuary is the only company, formerly producing stringholders, that is still in business.

Japan produced stringholders in the 1930's and again in more recent years. Stringholders marked "Hand Painted Japan", "Japan", and "Fred Hirode Japan" were made of ceramic in the 1930's.

In recent years, several ceramics companies in this country have made a few stringholders, but these are much less valuable to collectors then the chalkware stringholders of the past.

Chapter 1
IRON, CAST IRON, & GLASS

Here are a few examples of what most people think of when stringholders are mentioned. These predate the chalkware and ceramic stringholders, are harder to find, and usually cost more.

A large Beehive, cast iron stringholder.
$115

A small Beehive, cast iron stringholder.
$85

Cast iron stringholder.
$65

Ball of string holder, cast iron.
$125

Cast iron stringholder.
$65

Cast iron stringholder.
$65

Brass stringholder.
$85

Fancy cast iron stringholder.
$75

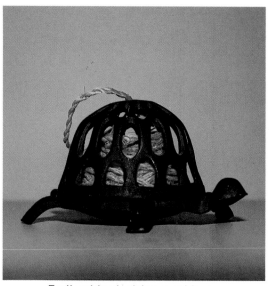

Turtle stringholder, cast iron.
$75

Cast aluminum tabletop stringholder.
$65

Blue Glass Bell.
$85

Peach Glass Bell.
$85

Green Glass Bell.
$85

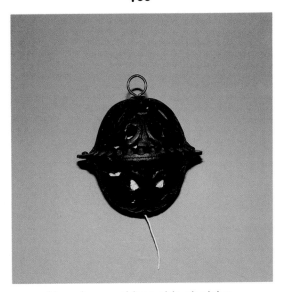

Hanging cast iron stringholder.
$65

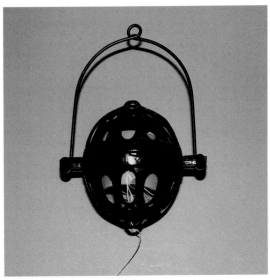

Hanging stringholder, cast iron.
$65

Hanging stringholder, brass.
$65

Wire stringholder and sack holder,
from a general store. – **$225**

Left: Oak & metal holder. Hung above counter.
Right: Metal holder. Hung above counter. –
$125 each

Balance stringholder from a general store.
$365

Old store-type steel stringholder.
$55

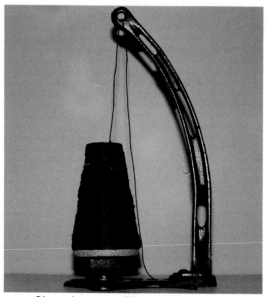

Store-type cast iron stringholder.
$70

Cast iron store-type stringholder.
$65

Store-type cast iron stringholder.
$65

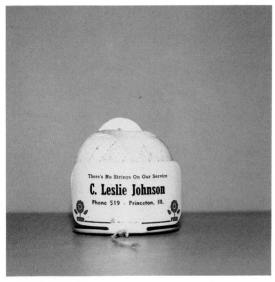

Advertising metal holder marked "There's No Strings on Our Service". – **$22**

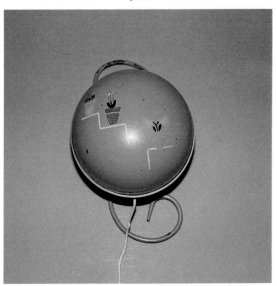

Enameled tin stringholder.
$40

Yarn holder, metal (both views shown).
$45

Floral painted tin stringholder.
$35

Metal Ball for holding yarn.
$35

Chicago Printed String Co., cast iron stringholder for department stores or dress shops.
$225

Chapter 2
Fruits & Vegetables

Many stringholders were made depicting fruits and vegetables, some with faces and some without. The fruits, especially the apples and the pears, are the most commonly seen stringholders and therefore the least expensive, with a few exceptions.

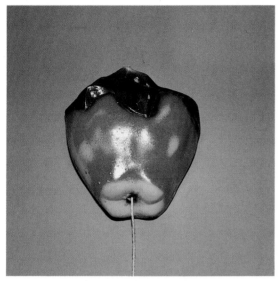

Apple stringholder, chalkware.
$32

Apple stringholder #887, chalkware.
$28

Apple and Cherries stringholder, chalkware.
$35

Apple stringholder, chalkware.
$28

Yellow Apple stringholder #887, chalkware.
$28

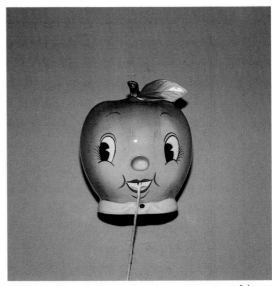

Apple with face, ceramic, Japan N.
$35

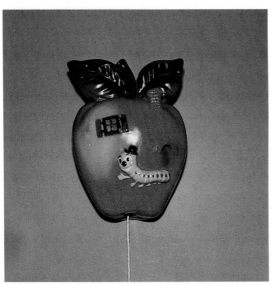

Apple with worm stringholder, chalkware.
$40

Apple stringholder, chalkware.
$28

Green Pepper, made of pressed paper.
$55

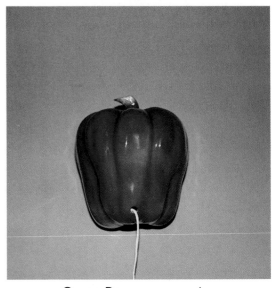

Green Pepper, ceramic.
$45

Peach stringholder, chalkware.
$37

Peach made of ceramic.
$40

Peach stringholder, chalkware.
$37

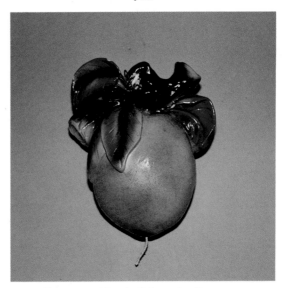

Orange stringholder, chalkware.
$50

Apple stringholder, chalkware. A Gallery copy,
R. Apply. – **$40**

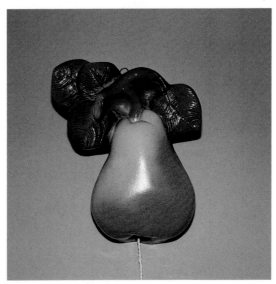

Pear stringholder, chalkware.
$30

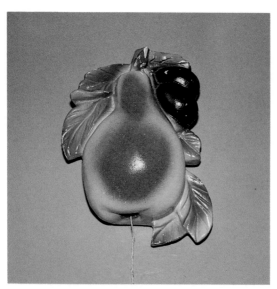

Pear stringholder, chalkware.
$28

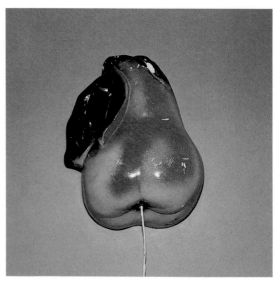

Pear stringholder, made of pressed paper.
$55

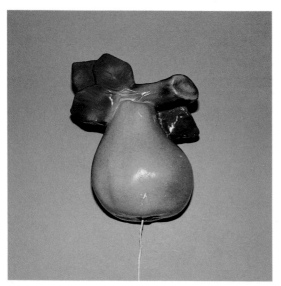

Pear stringholder, chalkware.
$32

Strawberry stringholder, chalkware.
$35

Strawberry stringholder, chalkware.
$40

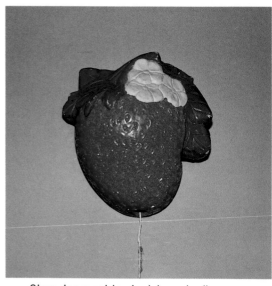

Strawberry stringholder, chalkware.
$35

Strawberry with a face, chalkware.
$45

Strawberry with a face, chalkware.
$45

Strawberry with pot holder hooks, chalkware.
Companion piece to picture at the right.

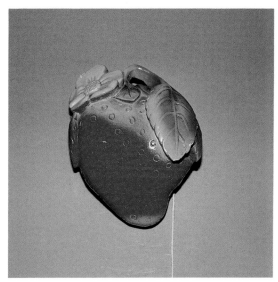

Strawberry stringholder, chalkware.
Companion to pot holder at left. – **$35**

Tomato Chef, made of ceramic.
$55

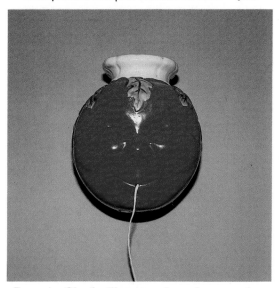

Tomato Chef with eyes closed, ceramic.
$55

Tomato stringholder, chalkware.
$40

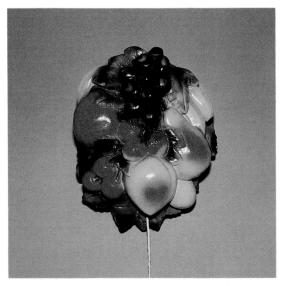

Bunch of Fruit stringholder, chalkware.
$45

Bananas, chalkware.
$55

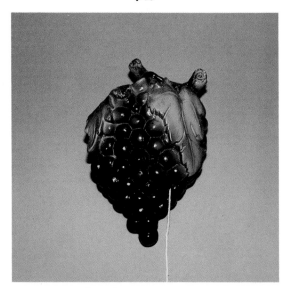

Grapes, chalkware.
$50

Cherries, chalkware.
$50

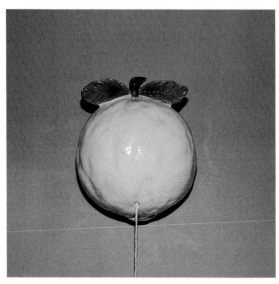

Lemon, ceramic.
$45

Pineapple with a face, chalkware.
$55

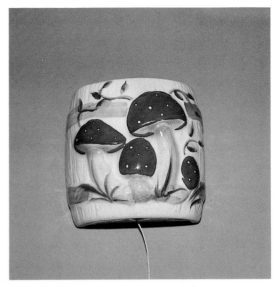
Mushrooms, ceramic.
$30

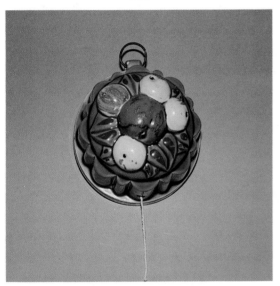
Plum Pudding, ceramic.
$45

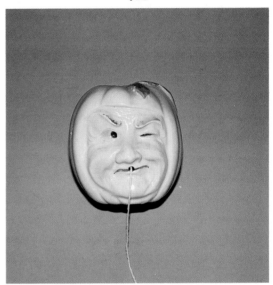
Winking Witch in a Pumpkin, ceramic.
$75

Cabbage, ceramic.
$40

Gourd, chalkware.
$70

Chapter 3
ANIMALS

Stringholders depicting animals were very popular. Cats and dogs were especially common as were birds and pigs. The section on animals is divided into specific animals to make comparison easier.

Cats

Cats were a real favorite, quite often depicted with a ball of string. Others had loops or bows which served as a handy spot to put a pair of small scissors for cutting string. Here you see four cats from the same mold painted to look completely different.

Cat on a Ball of String, ceramic.
$40

Cat with a Ball of String with chains, ceramic.
$40

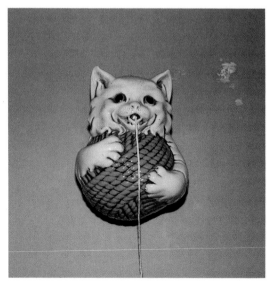

Cat on a Ball of String, ceramic.
$40

Cat with a Ball of String, ceramic.
$40

18

Cat with Scissor holder in bow,
ceramic, ©1958 Holt Howard. – **$40**

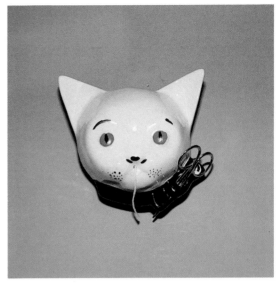

Cat with Scissors in holder on bow, ceramic.
$45

Cat with Scissors in holder on bow, ceramic.
$40

Cat with Scissors in holder on bow, ceramic.
$45

Cat with Scissors in holder on bow, ceramic.
$45

Cat with Scissors in holder on bow, ceramic.
$45

Cat with Scissors in holder on bow, ceramic.
$45

Cat on a Ball of String, chalkware.
$45

Cat on a Ball of String, chalkware.
$45

Cat on a Ball of String, ceramic.
$45

Cat on a Ball of String, ceramic.
$45

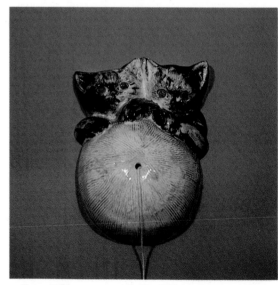

Two Kittens on a Ball of String, ceramic.
$45

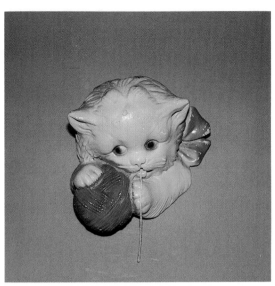

Kitten with a Ball of String, chalkware.
$45

Cat with Flowers and matching basket wall
pocket and stringholder. – **$60 for both**

Cat Face stringholder, ceramic.
$55

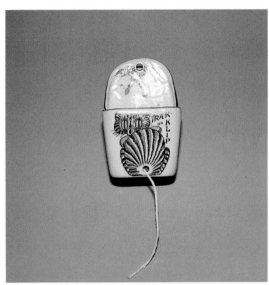

Cat stringholder, ceramic, imported.
$30

Cat with scissors, ceramic.
$40

Cat Head stringholder, ceramic.
$38

Cat stringholder, ceramic.
$45

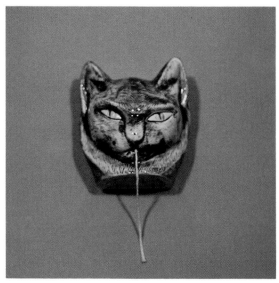

Cat stringholder, ceramic, marked Japan.
$60

Cat Head stringholder, chalkware.
$85

Handmade Cat stringholder, ceramic.
$45

Dogs

Fewer dogs than cats were made so their value is somewhat higher than their feline counterparts.

Dog in a Chef's Hat, chalkware.
$85

Bull Dog, chalkware.
$85

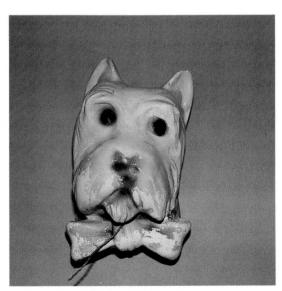

Westie, chalkware.
$85

Westie, chalkware.
$75

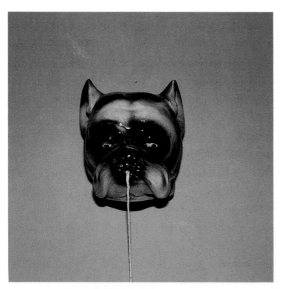

Boxer, ceramic.
$85

Scotty, ceramic, marked Japan.
$125

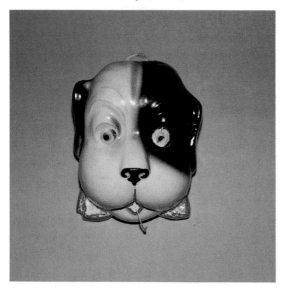

Dog with Bow, ceramic.
$85

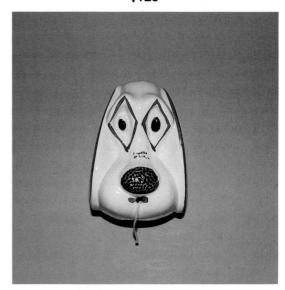

Dog Head, ceramic.
$55

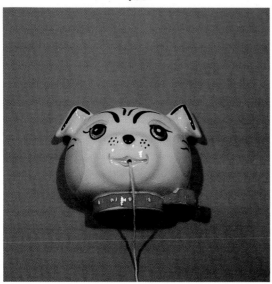

Dog with Scissor Holder in collar, ceramic.
Marked Royal Bradwell Ware. – **$50**

Dog with Scissor Holder in collar, ceramic.
$50

Dog with Scissor Holder in collar, ceramic.
(Can hang on wall or will stand).
$50

Dog with Scissor Hole in head, ceramic.
Marked Englishware USA, handpainted,
made in England.
$55

Dog with Scissors in Holder on collar.
(Can hang on wall or will stand).
$50

Birds

Birds were portrayed alone, in birdhouses, and in cages. A particularly sought-after bird is the Royal Bayreuth Rooster, made in Bavaria by Royal Bayreuth. It is valued at nearly $500.

This is the trademark they used after the 1900's, underglazed in blue, gray or gold. It was overglazed after 1902.

Rooster stringholder, ceramic. Marked Royal Bayreuth, Bavaria.
(four different views)
$350-500

Parrot, chalkware.
$75

Parrot, chalkware.
$75

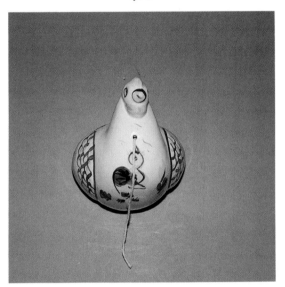

Dove, ceramic.
$45

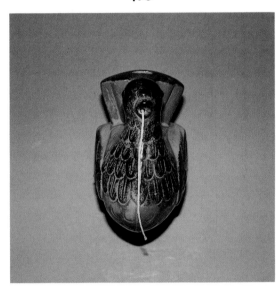

Bird, made of pottery.
$45

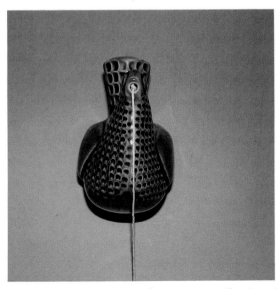

Bird, ceramic, marked Arthurwood, England.
$55

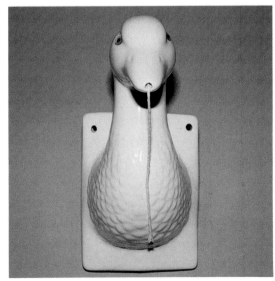

Goose, ceramic.
$35

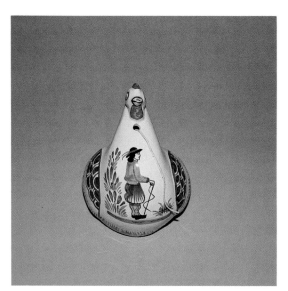

Bird, ceramic, marked Henriot Quimper, France.
$100

Owl, ceramic. By Mead Pottery, England with
Goose Logo. – **$55**

Owl, ceramic, by Mead Pottery, England.
$55

Owl with Scissor Holder in Nose, ceramic.
$45

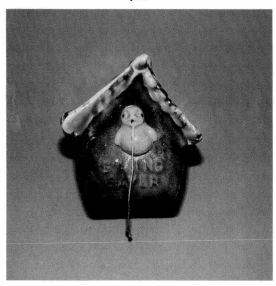

Bird in Birdhouse, pottery,
written under bird "String Saver". – **$50**

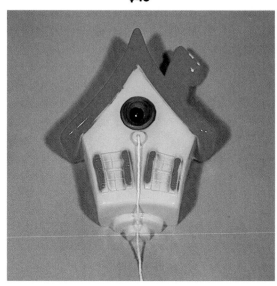

Bird in birdhouse, chalkware.
$55

Canary in Cage, small, chalkware.
$75

Two Canaries in a Cage, large, chalkware.
$80

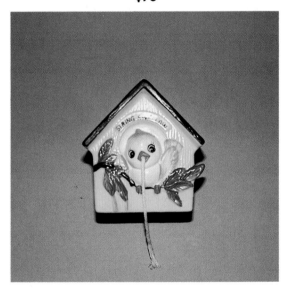

Swallow in a Birdhouse, ceramic.
$55

Bird Peeking out of a Birdhouse.
$55

Dove, ceramic.
$45

Bird Pulling A Worm from the Apple, chalkware.
$65

String Nest and Scissor Nest pair, ceramic.
$70 per pair

Birds on a Nest, made of clay or ceramic.
$120

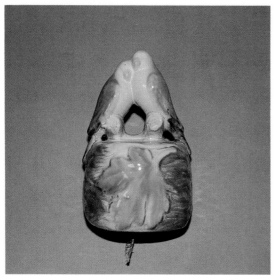

Birds on Nest, ceramic.
$55

Duck with Scissors in Holder, ceramic.
$45

Other Animals

"Posie the Pig" is shown in this section in its original box! Almost unheard of!

Monkeys

Here you see the "Monkey On A Ball of String" painted in four different colors from the factory.

Monkey on Ball of String, chalkware.
$65

Monkey on Ball of String, chalkware.
$65

Monkey on Ball of String, chalkware.
$65

Monkey on Ball of String, chalkware.
$65

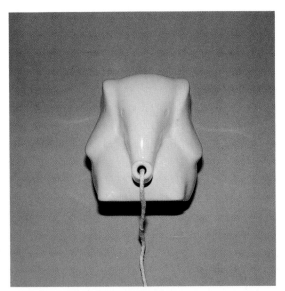

Elephant, ceramic, made in Heffritz, England.
$60

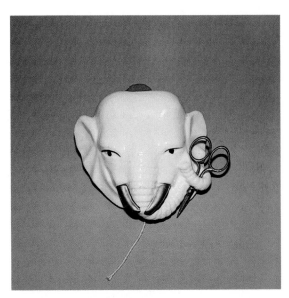

Elephant with Pincushion and Trunk
holding Scissors, ceramic. – **$60**

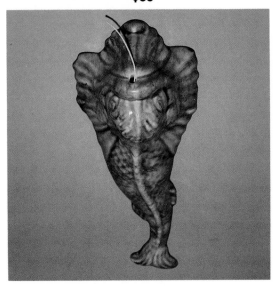

Fish, ceramic. Marked California Pottery,
Monterey Jade. – **$55**

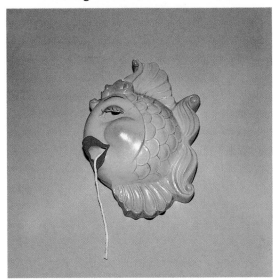

Goldfish, chalkware.
$80

Pig, ceramic.
$55

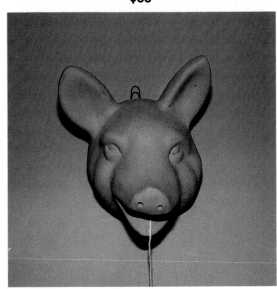

Pig, clay.
$65

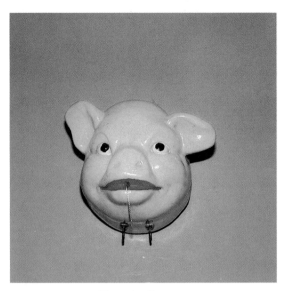

Pig, chalkware.
$70

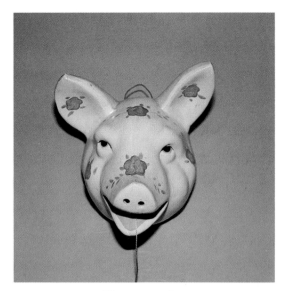

Pig, ceramic.
$65

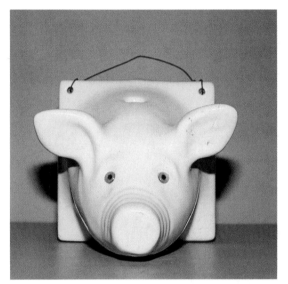

Pig with Scissor Hole, ceramic.
$35

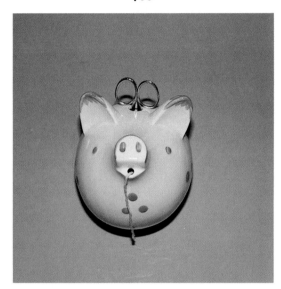

Pig with Scissors, ceramic, 1982.
Marked F.F. Japan. – **$35**

Posie Pig in original box, chalkware.
$85

Chipmunk with Scissor Holder in Bow, ceramic.
$45

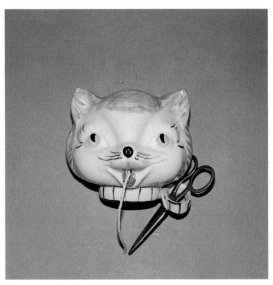

Fox with Scissors in Holder, handmade
by Ross, ceramic – **$65**

Bear with Scissors in Collar, ceramic.
$45

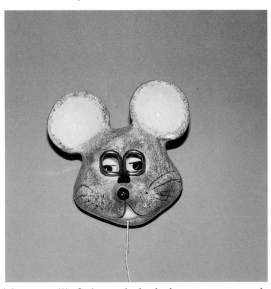

Mouse with Scissors in hole in nose, ceramic.
$50

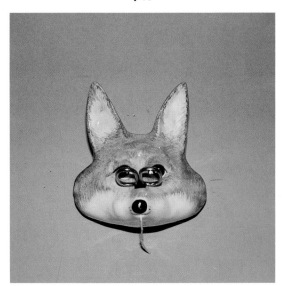

Fox with Scissors in hole in nose, ceramic,
marked Devon, England. – **$60**

Rabbit, chalkware.
$80

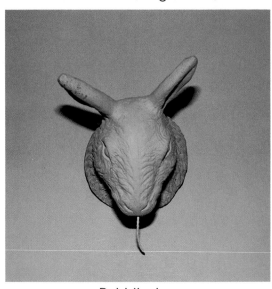

Rabbit, clay.
$75

34

Mouse, ceramic.
$60

Christmas Chipmunk, ceramic.
$55

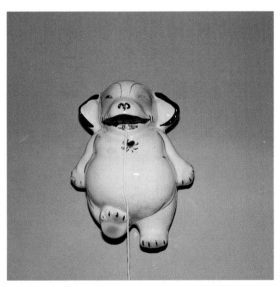

Bear with a Bee on its Chest,
marked with handmade, Japan.
$70

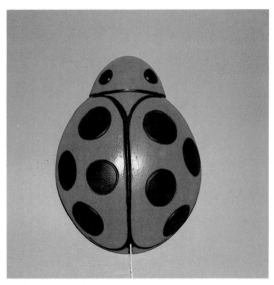

Ladybug, chalkware.
$50

$\mathcal{C}hapter\ 4$
HUMAN FACES

The most loved of all stringholders! From the very common to the extremely rare.

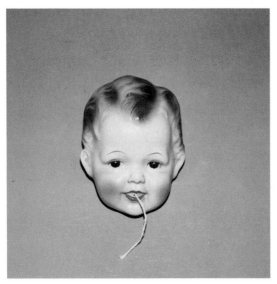

Baby Face, ceramic.
$45

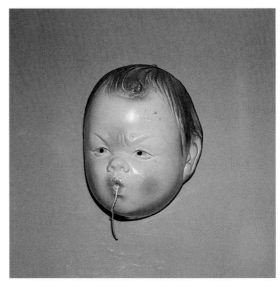

Baby Face, chalkware.
$250

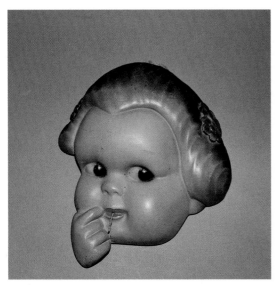

Girl (companion to boy at right), chalkware.
$60

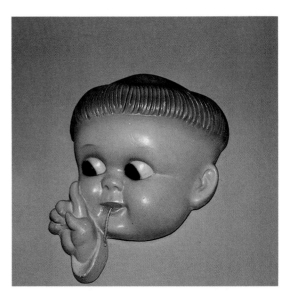

Boy (companion to Girl at left), chalkware.
$60

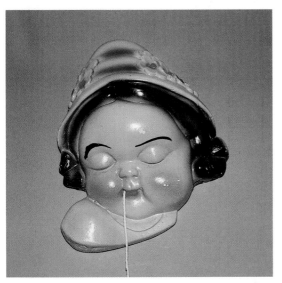

Sleeping Girl with Bonnet, chalkware. – **$45**
(Companion to boy pictured at right)

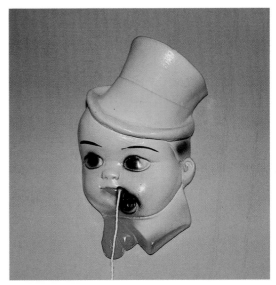

Boy with Top Hat and Pipe, chalkware. – **$45**
(Companion to girl pictured at left)

Boy with Top Hat and Pipe, chalkware. – **$45**
(Companion to girl pictured at right)

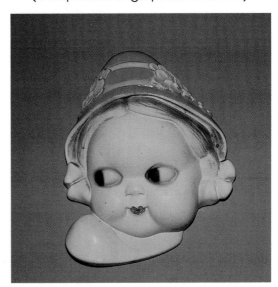

Girl in a Bonnet, chalkware. – **$45**
(Companion to boy pictured at left)

Winking Moon Face, chalkware. – **$85**
(Companion to moon pictured at right)

Moon Face Match Holder, chalkware. – $75
(Companion to winking moon pictured at left)

37

Clown Pulling Tooth, chalkware.
$65

Clown with String Tied Around Tooth, chalkware.
$65

Bozo The Clown, chalkware.
$60

Jester/Clown, small, chalkware.
$75

Jester/Clown with hole in top of head for
matches, chalkware. – **$60**

Jester/Clown, chalkware.
$60

38

Red Riding Hood, chalkware.
$65

Blue Riding Hood, chalkware.
$65

White Riding Hood, chalkware. By H. Bello
Universal Str. Co., ©1941. – **$65**

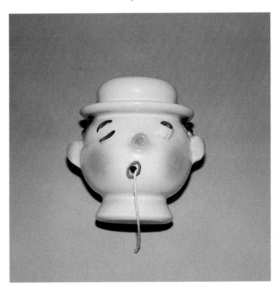

Drunk Man, ceramic, by Elsa.
$50

Man, marked "Just A Gigolo", chalkware.
$60

Chinaman, ceramic, made in Japan, No. 59528.
$65

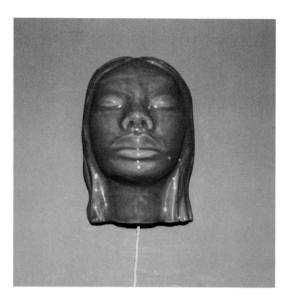

Woman's Head, ceramic.
$30

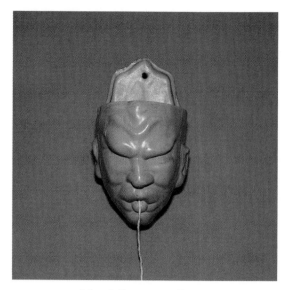

Man's Face, pottery.
$60

Chinaman, pressed plastic or resin.
$50

Father Christmas, ceramic.
$55

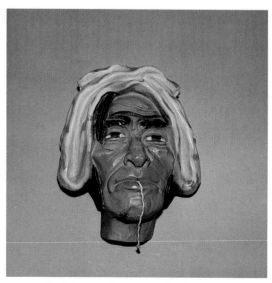

Robinson Crusoe, chalkware.
$65

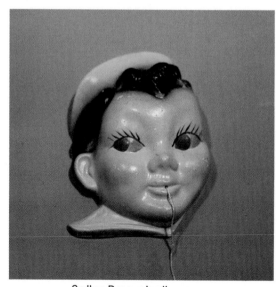

Sailor Boy, chalkware,
$65

Woman in scarf, chalkware.
$75

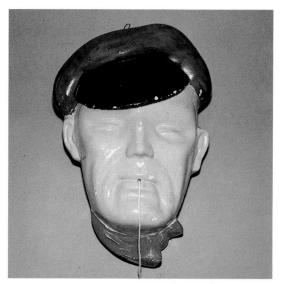

Longshoreman, chalkware.
$125

Sailor Boy, chalkware.
$65

Porter, chalkware.
$45

Gypsy, made of pressed paper.
$50

Pottery Face.
$40

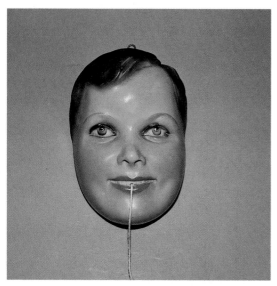

Young Man's Face, chalkware.
$65

Maid, ceramic. By Sasparilla Deco Designs, ©1984.
$40

Woman's Head, ceramic, marked Japan.
$55

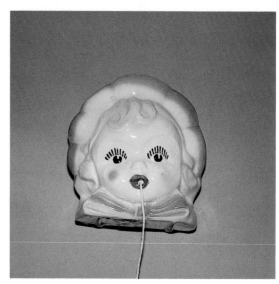

Girl in Bonnet, ceramic.
$55

Woman's Face, papier mache, Japan import.
$28

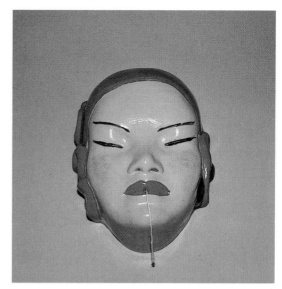

Asian Woman, chalkware.
$65

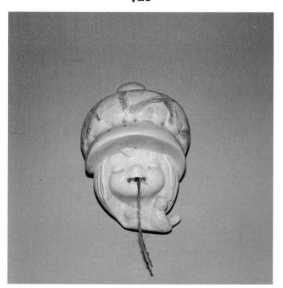

Mod Girl, ceramic.
$30

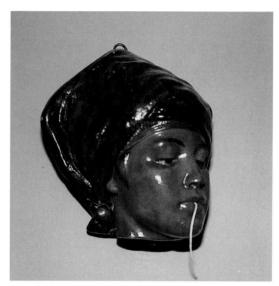

Woman with Turban, chalkware.
$75

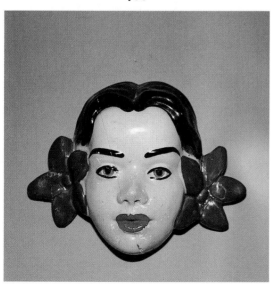

Hawaiian Girl, chalkware.
$55

Girl in a Winter Cap, ceramic.
$65

Famous Faces

It is surprising that stringholders were not often made depicting famous people and cartoon characters of the time. However, stringholders were made of Betty Boop and Shirley Temple. Both made in the 1930's, they are extremely rare and quite valuable. A ceramic reproduction of Betty Boop was made in 1985.

Original Betty Boop with shoulders, chalkware.
$300

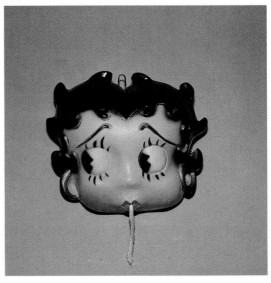

Original Betty Boop, chalkware.
$275

Betty Boop, ceramic, ©KFS 1985,
Vandor, made in Japan.
$45

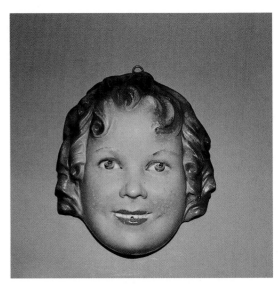

Shirley Temple, chalkware.
$225

Chefs

The most often-seen stringholder face. From the very common to the hard to find. A favorite for the kitchen.

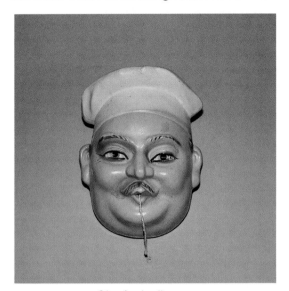

Chef, chalkware.
$65

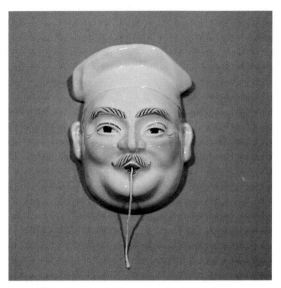

Chef, ceramic, made in Japan.
$60

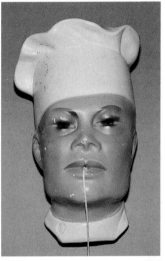

Chef, chalk.
$90

Chef with Rolling Pin, chalkware.
$65

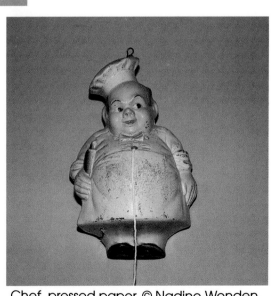

Chef, pressed paper, © Nadine Wenden,
1941, Made in U.S.A. – **$75**

Rice Crispy Guy, chalkware.
$75

Chef, very large, chalkware.
$85

Chef, ceramic.
$65

Chef with Pot Holder Hooks, chalkware.
$65

Chef, chalkware.
$70

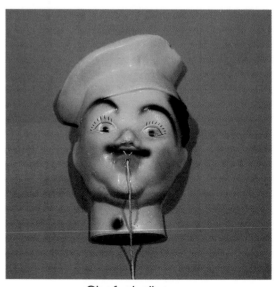

Chef, chalkware
$45

Chef, chalkware, © Conovers Original, 1945.
$75

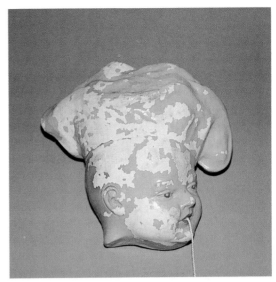

Baby Chef, chalkware.
$75 (in good condition)

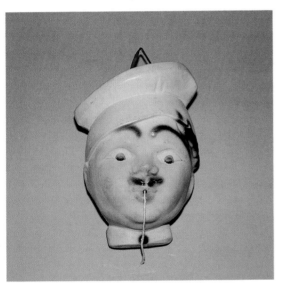

Chef, chalkware.
$55

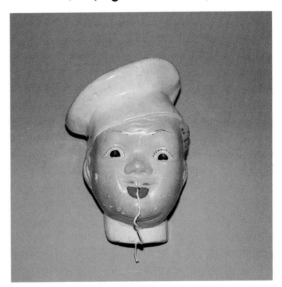

Chef, chalkware.
$55

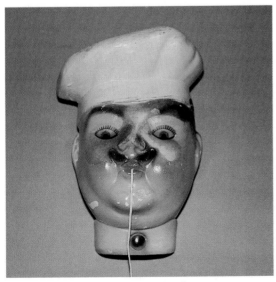

Chef, large size, chalkware.
$70

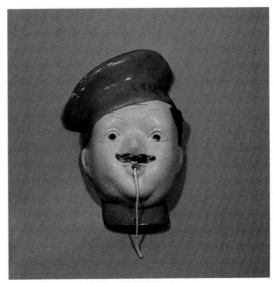

Chef, chalkware
$35

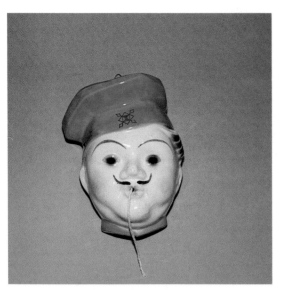

Chef, ceramic, made in Japan.
$55

Chef, ceramic.
$55

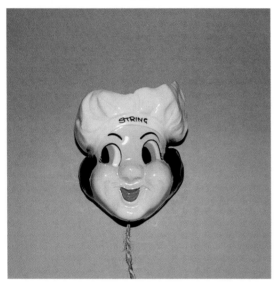

Woman Chef, ceramic, marked
handpainted, California. – **$60**

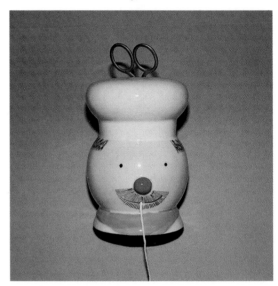

Chef with Scissors in Hat, ceramic.
$35

Bartender, ceramic, Hirode, Japan.
$75

Baker with Towel saying "String Saver", ceramic.
$45

Dutch Girls

The second most commonly found face is the Dutch Girl. From the ordinary to the unusual, at least one is in every stringholder collection. Although they come from the same mold, these four dutch girls are very different.

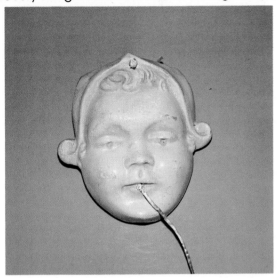

Dutch Girl, chalkware, open on Top of Head.
$65

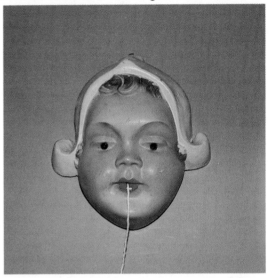

Common Dutch Girl, chalkware – **$40**

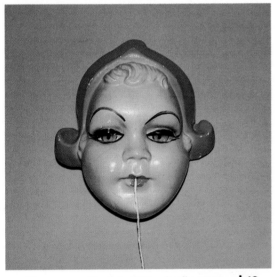

Common Dutch Girl, chalkware – **$40**

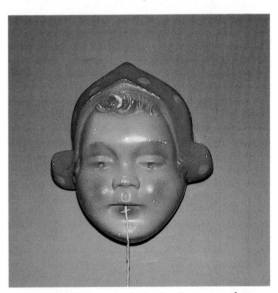

Common Dutch Girl, chalkware – **$40**

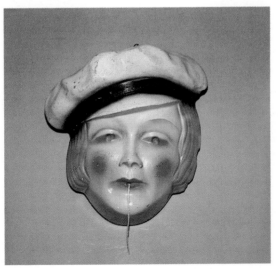

Dutch Boy, chalkware – **$60**

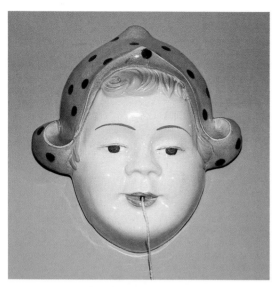

Dutch Girl, large, ceramic.
$65

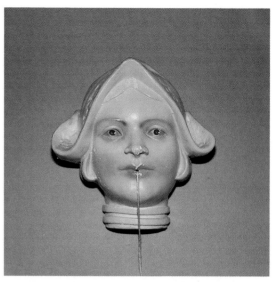

Dutch Girl, chalkware, Supreme Art
Novelty, Milwaukee, Wisc. – **$65**

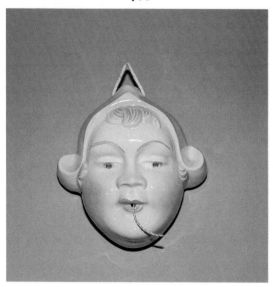

Dutch Girl, ceramic, Japan.
$55

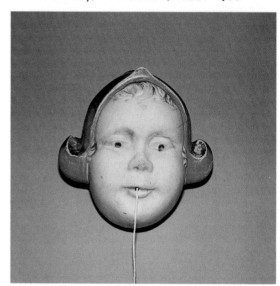

Dutch Girl, chalkware.
$65

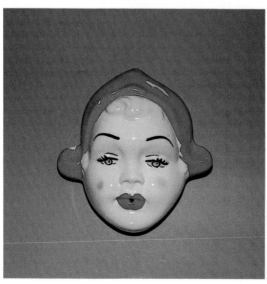

Dutch Girl, ceramic.
$45

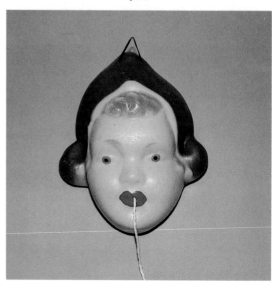

Dutch Girl, chalkware.
$60

W.W. II

Faces of soldiers, sailors, and "Rosie the Riveter", a female factory worker were made during W.W.II.

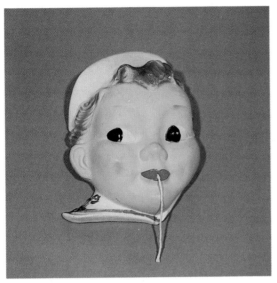

Sailor Boy, chalkware.
$65

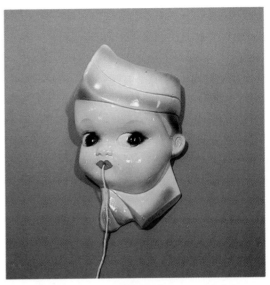

Soldier Boy, chalkware, by MAPCO.
$60

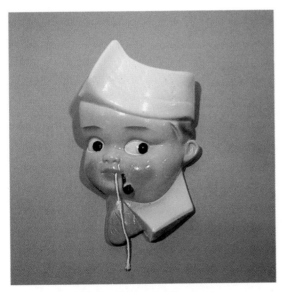

Soldier Boy, chalkware.
$60

Rosie The Riveter, chalkware.
$60

Chapter 5
BLACKS

Black memorabilia is highly collectible today largely for its historical significance. Stringholders, as well as many other household items, were made to portray blacks in a humorous or charming way. Since blacks are so collectible today, they are also priced quite high, accounting for the three-figure market values of black stringholders.

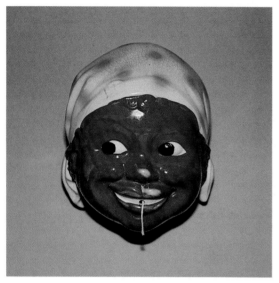

Mammy Face, ceramic.
$250

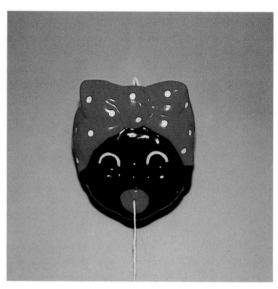

Mammy, ceramic.
$185

Black Couple, chalkware.
$200 per pair

Girl with Scarf, chalkware.
$250

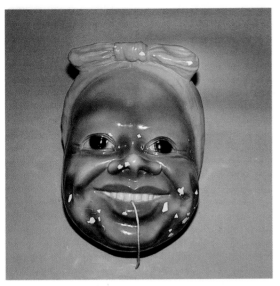

Mammy Face, chalkware, ©1947.
Ball of string fits on wire in back. – **$275**

Chef, chalkware.
$185

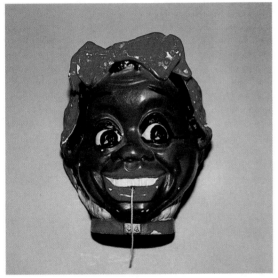

Mammy, chalkware. Inscription inside says,
"Glue an old razor blade in my bow". – **$275**

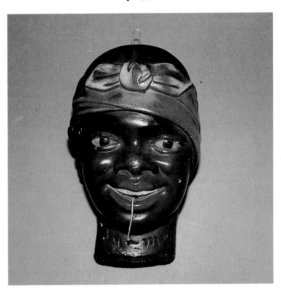

Mammy Face, chalkware, by Ty-me.
$225

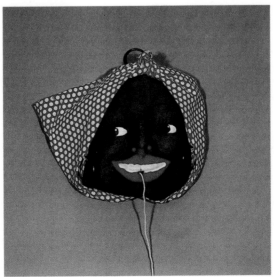

Mammy, cloth, rare.
$210

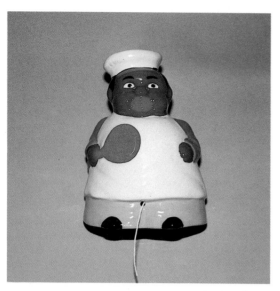

Chef, ceramic, (new – reproduction).
$50

Mammy Face, ceramic (reproduction).
$50

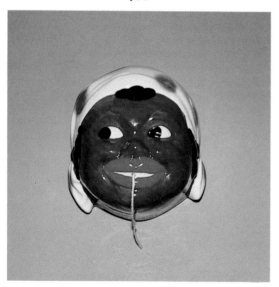

Mammy, ceramic, (reproduction).
$50

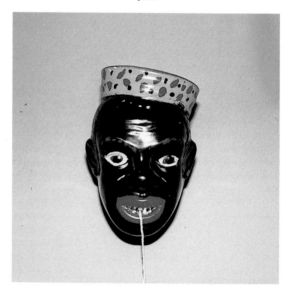

Porter, pottery, by Fredericksburg
Art Pottery, U.S.A. – **$185**

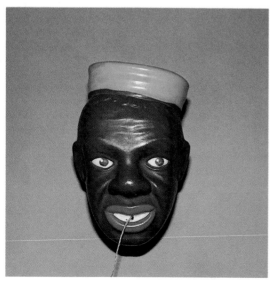

Porter, pottery, by Fredericksburg
Art Pottery, U.S.A. - **$185**

Black Girl, ceramic.
$210

Mammy with Scissors in Pocket, ceramic.
$185

Chef holding salt, chalkware.
$195

Baker, chalkware.
$195

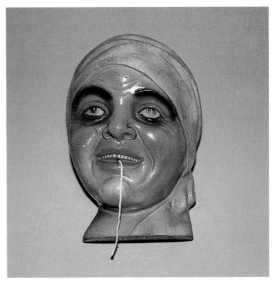

Mammy, chalkware.
$225

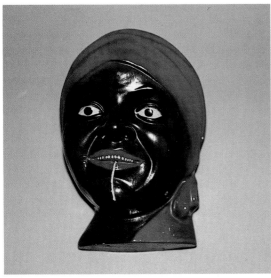

Mammy Face, chalkware.
$225

Mammy, chalkware.
$250

Mammy Face, chalkware, a Conover Original.
$250

Mammy, chalkware.
$195

Mammy, ceramic.
$175

Mammy, ceramic.
$185

Mammy, ceramic.
$185

Mammy, ceramic.
$185

Mammy, ceramic, made in Japan.
$165

Mammy, ceramic, made in Japan.
$150

Mammy (large version), made in Japan.
$175

Mammy, ceramic.
$175

Mammy, ceramic.
$185

Mammy, ceramic.
$185

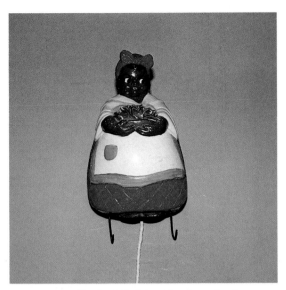

Mammy with Pot Holder Hooks, chalkware.
$195

Mammy with Laundry, chalkware.
$195

Mammy Holding Ball of String, 1947, chalkware.
$195

Mammy Holding Ball of String, cast iron.
$225

Mammy with Flowers, ceramic, made in Japan.
$185

Mammy with Flowers, ceramic, Hirode, Japan.
$185

Chapter 6
INDIANS

Some of the most charming stringholders portray Native Americans. Relatively few were made and thus are a "real find" and more expensive than some other human faces.

Indian Chief, chalkware.
$90

Indian Chief, ceramic.
$65

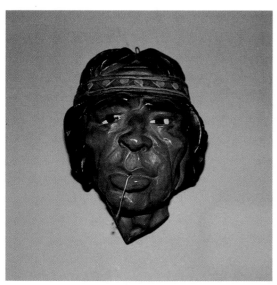

Indian, chalkware.
$80

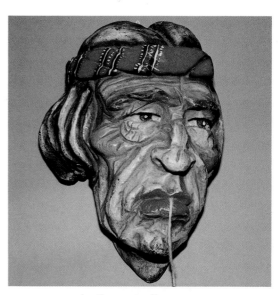

Indian, chalkware.
$85

Chapter 7
MEXICANS

My favorite stringholders are the beautiful senoras and the handsome senors, apparently sold most often in pairs. The senor is seen with his sombrero over his left eye, but a senor with a sombrero over his right eye was also made and is quite difficult to find. A smaller version of the common senor can be found, but I have never seen a senora to go with him. There are also several "banditos" which are also difficult to find.

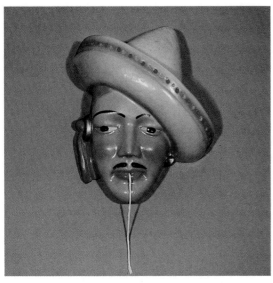

Senor, chalkware. – **$45**
(Companion to Senora pictured at right)

Senora, chalkware. – **$45**
(Companion to Senor pictured at left)

Senor, chalkware. – **$45**
(Companion to Senora pictured at right)

Senora, chalkware. – **$45**
(Companion to Senor pictured at left)

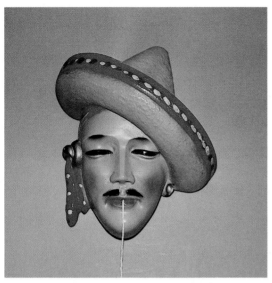

Senor, chalkware. – **$45**
(Companion to Senora pictured at right)

Senora, chalkware, by Universal Statuary Co.,
© 1947 – **$45** (Companion to Senor at left)

Pancho Villa, chalkware.
$60

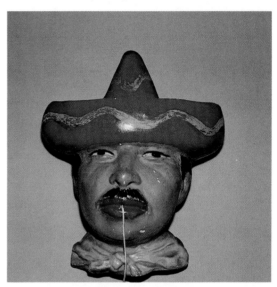

Bandito, chalkware.
$60

Senor, small, chalkware.
$45

Senor with Hat over right eye, unusual,
chalkware. – **$75**

61

Senora, chalkware.
$55

Senorita, chalkware.
$55

Senora, chalkware.
$55

Senora, chalkware.
$65

Chapter 8
FULL-FIGURES

As well as human faces, many stringholders were made to depict an entire human figure with the string hidden behind a full skirt or a portly midsection. A favorite among collectors is what is referred to as "The Bridal Party", consisting of a single "bride" in chalk or ceramic, a "bride" with two "bridesmaids" and a "groom" with two "bridesmaids", usually seen in ceramic.

Bride, chalkware.
$60

Bride, ceramic, made in Japan.
$55

Groom and Bridesmaids, ceramic, Japan.
$65

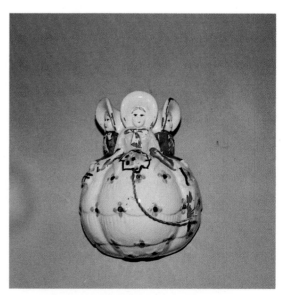

Bride and Bridesmaids, ceramic,
handpainted, Japan.
$65

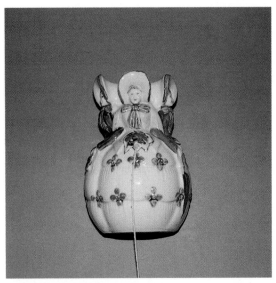

Bride and Bridesmaids, ceramic, Japan.
$65

My Kitchen Prayer.
$200

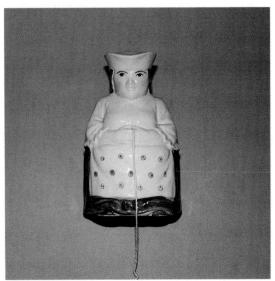

Peasant Woman, ceramic.
$75

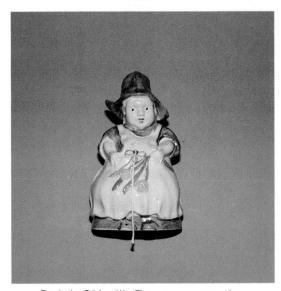

Dutch Girl with Flowers, ceramic.
$80

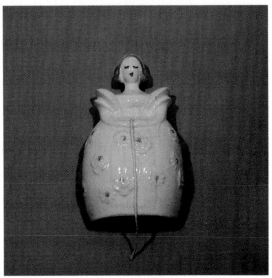

Woman in Flowered Dress, ceramic.
$50

Girl In A Chair, ceramic, made in Japan.
$65

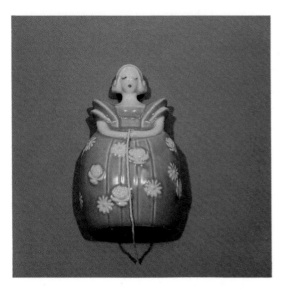

Woman in Flowered Dress, ceramic.
$50

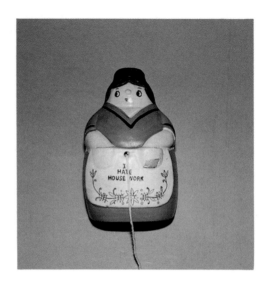

Housewife, ceramic.
$35

Cook with a place in the
top for scissors, ceramics. – **$30**

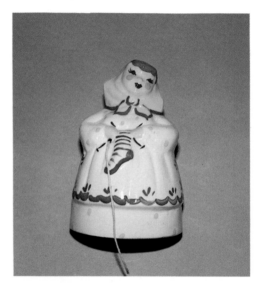

Peasant Woman Knitting, ceramic,
(has an unreadable label on bottom). – **$60**

Granny Sewing In A Rocking Chair, ceramic.
$55

Girl in a Sun Bonnet with a
Watering Can, ceramic. – **$40**

Clown with Scissor in hand, ceramic.
$35

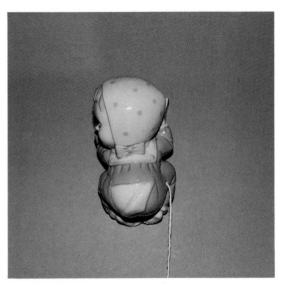

Sleeping Baby, ceramic, label on bottom
reads "Fine Quality, Lego, Japan.
$60

Victorian Girl, ceramic, Japan.
$65

Chapter 9
MISCELLANEOUS

Stringholders came in many shapes, defying any easy type of categorization.

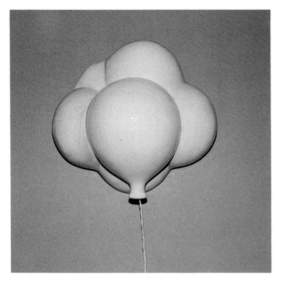

Balloons, ceramic, marked CFF 1983.
$40

Balloon, ceramic.
$35

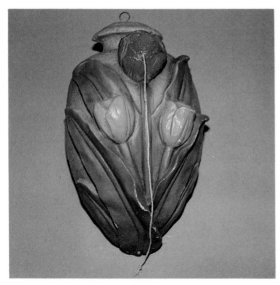

Tulips, chalkware.
$65

Rose, chalkware.
$40

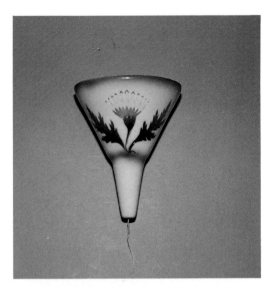

Funnel with Thistle design, ceramic.
$75

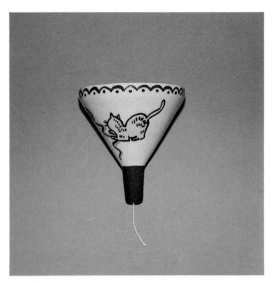

Funnel, ceramic, marked "Stringholder" inside.
$60

Heart, ceramic marked "You'll always
have a pull with me". – **$55**

Heart, ceramic, marked "String along
with me", handpainted, California. – **$55**

Heart, ceramic, marked "String Along
With Me", made in California. – **$55**

Heart, ceramic, "Men Make Houses, Women
Make Homes", by Arthur Wood, England – **$60**

House, ceramic, © California Cleminsons, handpainted. – **$55**

House with Welcome Sign and Scissors, ceramic. – **$35**

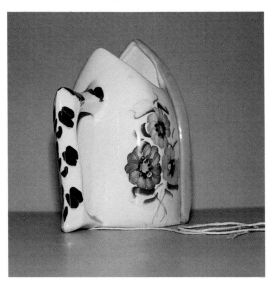

Iron, ceramic.
$70

Advertising Stringholder, marked J.P. Combs Crockery, made by Moire Pottery Co. Ltd. England. – **$70**

Flower Pot and Measuring Spoons, ceramic.
$35

Ball of String, chalkware.
$55

Teapot, ceramic.
$60

Donkey and Cactus, clay pottery.
$30

Chapter 10
CLOTH AND WOOD

Some stringholders made of cloth and/or wood are examples of homemade craft projects from the 1930's and 40's, much like the oatmeal box stringholders. Collectors of primitives are also interested in these charming handicrafts.

Rabbit, wood, made in Germany.
$65

Woman, wood (two pieces).
$65

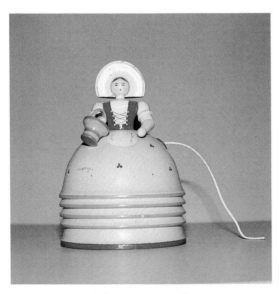

Woman, wood.
$65

Birdhouse, wood.
$40

71

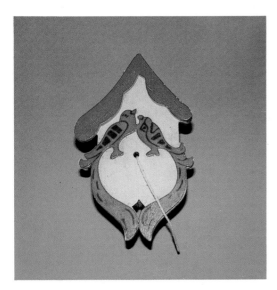

Birdhouse, wood.
$40

Birdhouse, wood, by M.G. Japan.
$40

Store type stringholder, wood.
$75

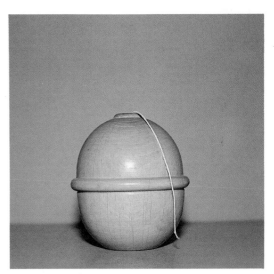

Wooden stringholder.
$45

Teapot with Black Chef decal. Made of
wood. By A.J. Wurts Creation, Pat. Pend. – **$75**

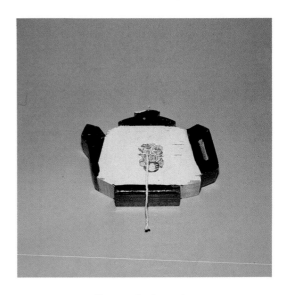

Teapot, wood.
$40

72

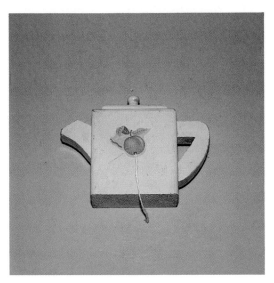

Teapot, wood.
$40

Farmer, made of cloth.
$35

Cat, made of wood and cloth.
$40

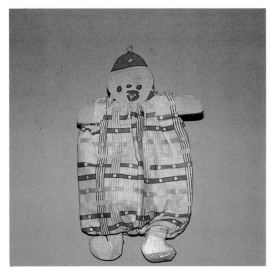

Clown, wood and cloth.
$40

Black girl, wood and cloth.
$45

Mammy, cloth and wood.
$45

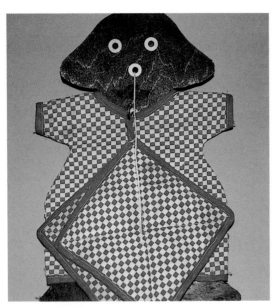

Black Child, wood and cloth. Also has
a potholder hook. – **$45**

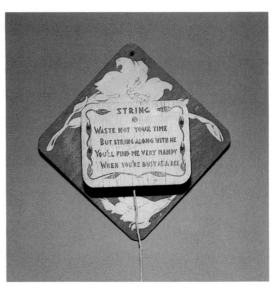

Wood stringholder, (with poem).
$45

Dutch Girl, wood.
$50

Pansies, wood.
$35

Dog stringholder, wood.
$35

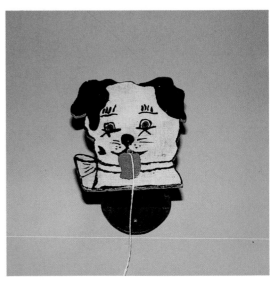

Dog stringholder, wood.
$35

Girl In A Garden, wood.
$45

Flower decal on wood stringholder.
$30

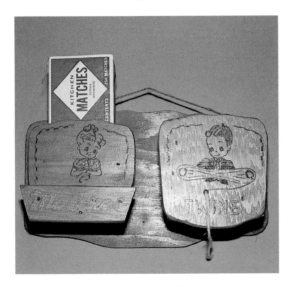

Match and twine holder, wood.
$40

Sally Stringholder, made of Aspen wood
in Mackinaw City, Michigan. – **$40**

Humpty Dumpty, wood.
$45

For Victory Farmers "String Along with Us For
Highest Cream Prices", wood. – **$50**

75

$\mathcal{C}$hapter 11
OATMEAL BOXES

Back when people seldom threw out anything, oatmeal boxes became children's drums, storage containers, and pretty stringholders in the kitchen. A hand-stitched face was secured over the bottom of a cut-off oatmeal box and adorned with a frilly bonnet and bows. Cottage cheese containers were also used in this way. Shown here are rare examples of oatmeal boxes with chalk faces instead of the hand-stitched variety.

Girl in Bonnet, cloth with a chalk face, unusual.
$85

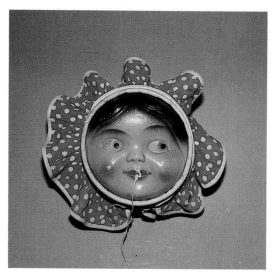

Girl in Bonnet, cloth with a chalk face, unusual.
$85

Girl in a Bonnet, cloth.
$45

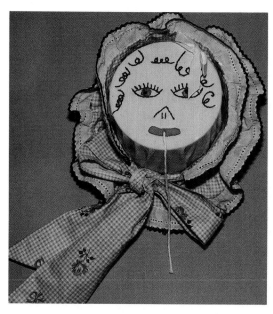

Girl in a Bonnet, cloth.
$45

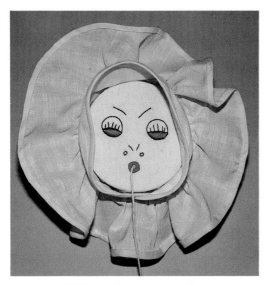

Girl in a Bonnet, cloth.
$40

Girl in a Bonnet, cloth.
$45

Girl in a Bonnet, cloth.
$45

Girl in a Bonnet, cloth.
$40

Girl in a Bonnet, cloth.
$40

Girl in a Bonnet, cloth, homemade.
$45

Girl in a Bonnet, cloth, with a painted face.
$40

Mammy in Bonnet, cloth.
$75

Stringholder made from an Ice Cream
Container, covered with wallpaper.
$15

Chapter 12
COCONUTS

Stringholders made from coconuts are mostly seen depicting mammys. Apparently they were sold in souvenir shops in areas where coconuts normally grow. Some are made in Mexico and sold as small mask-like wall decorations, but they make a great stringholder! The example here of the "Organ-Grinder's Monkey", made of a coconut and chalkware is quite unusual.

Mammy
$40

Coconut and chalkware face, Mexico. – **$40**

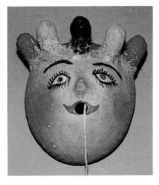

Coconut and chalkware face, mexican.
$25

Organ Grinder Monkey, chalk on a coconut.
$75

Mammy
$35

Mammy, Trinidad, BWI.
$38

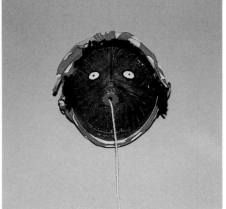

Mammy
$35

Chapter 13
COUNTER-TOP

Most decorative stringholders were made to hang on the wall, but quite a few were made to stand on the kitchen counter. Most counter-tops are more recently made, but there are some older ones shown here.

Kitchen String, ceramic. By Burleigh Ironstone, Staffordshire, England.
$55

Kitchen Twine, tin and paper. Hoan Products Ltd., Ramsey, NJ 07446 – No. 753.
$45

Advertising Plastic stringholder. Marked "Friendship Ties, Quickle Sales and Service, Sheffield."
$35

Plastic stringholder.
$20

Bakelite stringholder.
$65

Advertising "Clark's – Glace Finish, O.N.T. Left
Twist Four Cord (50), 6,000 yds." – **$45**

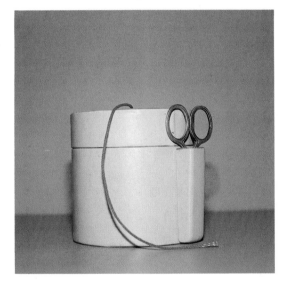

Leather box stringholder with scissors in holder.
$30

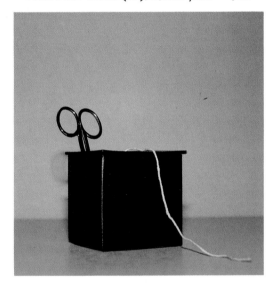

Leather box stringholder with scissors in holder.
$30

Yarn holder, plastic. By Sommer Mfg. Co.,
Newark, NJ – **$45**

Yarn holder, plastic. By Sommer Mfg. Co.,
Newark, NJ – **$45**

Humpty Dumpty, ceramic.
$110

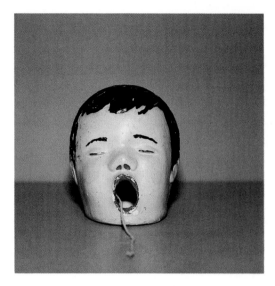

Yawning Baby, chalkware.
$55

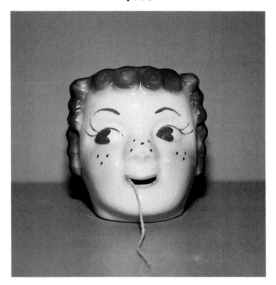

Girl's head, ceramic.
$45

Owl with scissors in holder, ceramic.
By Clover Industries. – **$30**

Rooster, two piece, ceramic.
$40

Duck with scissors in holder, ceramic.
$28

Frog with scissors in holder – two pieces,
ceramic. By Omnibus, Japan – **$30**

Rabbit, ceramic.
$55

Woman's Head, ceramic.
By Hemisphere Corp. K.C., MS – **$35**

Granny Knitting, ceramic.
$40

Shmoo, ceramic, by Babbacombe,
Devon, England. – **$45**

Dog, ceramic, marked Knitter's Pal, ©1952. By
Palm Springs Ceramics Fortuna, California – **$35**

Witch with scissors in holder,
ceramic. By Fitz & Floyd. – **$35**

Chef with scissors in holder, ceramic.
by Fitz & Floyd Inc. MCMLXXX, FF. – **$30**

Frog with scissors in holder, ceramic.
By Babbacombe, Devon, England. – **$35**

Hippo Knitting with scissor in holder, ceramic.
Made by Babbacombe, Devon, England. – **$40**

Mouse, ceramic, Japan.
$35

Woman holding scissors, ceramic, two pieces.
By Fitz & Floyd, Inc. – **$35**

Kangaroo Knitting with scissors in holder,
ceramic, homemade. – **$25**

Cat and Ball of String, ceramic, two pieces.
By Fitz & Floyd, Co., MCMLXXX, FF. – **$30**

Cat and Mouse, ceramic, two pieces.
Marked Quon-Quon MCMLXXX, Japan. – **$30**

Beehive, ceramic.
$30

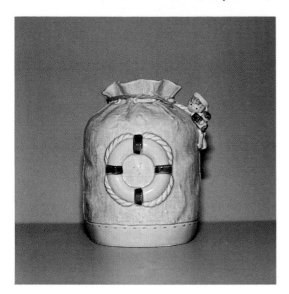

Dufflebag, ceramic, E-9210 ©1977, by Enesco.
$35

Pig with scissors in holder, ceramic, Japan.
$30

Cat with string, ceramic. By Takahashi
San Francisco, handpainted.
$30

Jonah and The Whale, ceramic, two pieces.
By Fitz & Floyd.
$35

Chef's Head, ceramic, two pieces.
$35

Chapter 14
FAKES?

Many times a collector will find a "stringholder" that upon closer inspection discovers that it is a wall plaque that has been cleverly hollowed out in the back and drilled for the string to come out of the mouth. Collectors should be aware of this and carefully inspect each purchase.

One can usually tell by the heavier weight of the wall plaque and by the rough, "after-the-fact" appearance of the drilled hole. It can be argued that these are stringholders now, but for the purist they are still wall plaques.

Other common misnomers are the pineapple and apple wall lamps. When the lamp hardware is removed, the opening for the lamp cord is mistaken for a string hole!

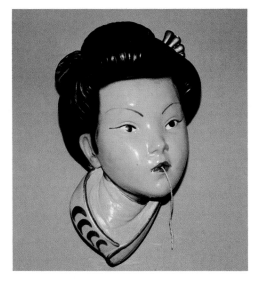

Chinese Woman, chalkware, wall plaque.

Chinese Man, chalkware, wall plaque.

Masked Man, chalkware, wall plaque.

Masked Woman, chalkware, wall plaque.

Siamese Face, chalkware.

Woman's Head, chalkware.

Indian Pottery Head.

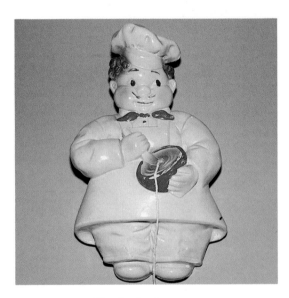

Chef, chalkware.

Pineapple Lamp, commonly mistaken for a stringholder when lamp parts are removed.